Marketing Plans
in a week

ROS JAY

Hodder & Stoughton

A MEMBER OF THE HODDER HEADLINE GROUP

Orders: please contact Bookpoint Ltd, 130 Milton Park, Abingdon, Oxon OX14 4SB. Telephone: (44) 01235 827720, Fax: (44) 01235 400454. Lines are open from 9.00 - 6.00, Monday to Saturday, with a 24 hour message answering service. Email address: orders@bookpoint.co.uk

British Library Cataloguing in Publication Data
A catalogue record for this title is available from The British Library

ISBN 0 340 849576

First published 1997
Impression number   10   9   8   7   6   5   4   3   2   1
Year   2007 2006 2005 2004 2003

Cover image: Stone/Getty Images

Typeset by SX Composing DTP, Rayleigh, Essex
Printed in Great Britain for Hodder & Stoughton Educational, a division of Hodder Headline Plc, 338 Euston Road, London NW1 3BH by Cox & Wyman Ltd, Reading, Berkshire.

C O N T E N T S

Marketing is the lifeblood of any business. You may have a great product, loads of technical know-how and years of experience in financial management. But if you want your business to thrive – let alone grow – you need good, sound marketing. And the first and most crucial step towards that is the marketing plan.

Many business people think they can get away without a marketing plan. Many others try not to think about it at all, because secretly they haven't really got a clue what it is or how to put one together.

But the best and most successful businesses have a clear and thorough plan. What's more, it doesn't live buried somewhere at the bottom of a filing cabinet; it's one of their most useful tools and they refer to it frequently. A really good marketing plan will make it far easier for you to run your business smoothly and effectively.

Some businesses may fail to recognise the value of marketing planning, but the banks and financial institutions don't make the same mistake. A business that tries to apply for a loan or a grant without a good marketing plan is unlikely to get very far.

This book explains how to draw up the kind of marketing plan that will impress the bank manager. The vital stages it covers are:

Sunday	What is a marketing plan?
Monday	Asking questions
Tuesday	Researching the answers
Wednesday	The objectives
Thursday	Converting objectives into action plans
Friday	Putting the plan together
Saturday	Using the marketing plan

What is a marketing plan?

So what exactly is a marketing plan? What goes into it? What does it look like? How long does it take to put one together?

We'll spend today answering all these practical questions, so that once we start drawing up the plan, you'll know what you're trying to achieve.

Essentially, a marketing plan is like a route map for your business. And it should cover three basic areas:

- Where you are
- Where you are going
- How you are going to get there

Where you are

If you're working out a route on a route map, you have to know where you're starting from before you can work out the best way to reach your destination. So the first stage of drawing up the marketing plan involves establishing precisely where your business is now.

It doesn't matter whether you're just starting up a business or whether you've been in business for a while. You need a marketing plan that starts from *now*.

The first part of the marketing plan establishes your current position. There are certain things that it needs to include:

- Information about your product or service
- Information about your customers and prospects
- Information about your competitors
- Information about your business

This is a very useful exercise for you to go through. You might imagine that since you obviously know where you are, it's rather pointless to waste time writing it down. But this isn't the case.

You'll be surprised how many things you don't know that you will have to go and find out – we'll be looking at this in more detail on Monday and Tuesday. What's more, going through this process helps you to home in on certain aspects of your marketing operation that you might not have given attention to otherwise. It brings weaknesses and opportunities into sharp focus.

You also need to establish at the start of your marketing plan precisely where you are because other people may want to know. The bank manager for a start, anyone you apply to for a loan or go to for advice, a new business partner, and so on. Having the information set out in black and white will turn out to be useful for all sorts of reasons.

This process of taking stock of your position before you start to think about your goals will help prevent mistakes later on. And mistakes can sometimes be expensive. Here's an example:

One of the things you will do when you establish where your business is now, is to analyse your weaknesses. Perhaps you will discover that apart from the directors or most senior managers, no one else in the business is very good at taking on important responsibilities.

Now suppose that a customer places a huge order. You accept it eagerly, but it's far too big to handle without delegating a lot of the work and responsibility to someone more junior. But hang on – you haven't got anyone you can confidently delegate it to.

This kind of situation can create huge muddle and expense to put right. If only you'd started training up your staff a year ago, ready to handle large orders by themselves if need be.

You might think that it would have been obvious from the start that there was no one in the company to whom you could delegate this sort of order. But in fact, this is the kind of mistake that companies often make, unfortunately.

Of course it was obvious from the start, *if* you thought about it. But all too often, you don't think about it. The process of drawing up a marketing plan helps you to focus on exactly this sort of potential mistake in time to avert trouble.

You'll see on Monday and Tuesday that the way you go about putting together this section of the marketing plan is to ask yourself lots of questions – we'll be looking at how you find out which questions to ask.

And then you go and find the answers – it's as simple as that. Once again, we'll be going into more detail about where and how to find the answers.

Where you are going

We've already established that you can't work out your route if you don't know where you're starting from. It's equally difficult if you don't know where you're going. So this section of the marketing plan sets out where you are trying to get to. There are three main stages in this part of the process:

- Identify your critical success factors
- Set your objectives
- Draw up a sales forecast

Identifying your critical success factors

First, you need to establish the factors which are critical to your success. Which things have you absolutely got to get right in order to succeed and grow? It may not be the end of the world, in some lines of business, if your prices are not particularly competitive – for example if you sell top of the range designer clothing. But if you run an office stationery business and you can't match your competitors' prices, you could go out of business as a result. So you will need to work out which aspects of your business or service are critical.

Establishing your marketing objectives

This is where you state your objectives. You will need to draw heavily on the first part of your plan to do this, which is yet another reason for having put down where you are now in black and white.

For example, the first part of your plan may have drawn your attention to a new type of product you could add to your range. So your objectives may include developing this product. Or the first section of the plan may have highlighted weaknesses that you want to eliminate – this would then be one of your objectives.

Objectives can be both large and small. The examples above might be relatively small things. You might also have objectives for expanding the business, which you will need to set out. Are you planning to open three new branches next year? Or franchise out the operation? Or employ your own sales force instead of using agents? These are all large objectives that need to be stated in your marketing plan.

You will also need to refer to your critical success factors to establish some of these objectives. If you're running an office stationery business, it may be a crucial objective to be able to match your competitors' prices on all frequently ordered products.

Sales forecast
This is the part of your marketing plan where you need to include your sales forecast. A lot of people find this bit some-what unnerving, since they don't really know how to forecast sales. They feel they are plucking numbers from the air.

However, there are techniques, which we will examine on Wednesday, for removing a lot of the guesswork from this process. Of course there are still some gaps that you will have to fill in with educated guesses, but you can go a long way towards an accurate forecast once you know how.

How you are going to get there

You have established where you are, and you've identified where you want to get to. This final section of the marketing plan explains how you plan to get from A to B. In other words, it states how you plan to achieve your objectives. This section is, in essence, your marketing strategy. In other words, it is the bit of the marketing plan which contains precise tasks and specific targets.

At this stage, it sounds to most people like an insurmountable challenge to draw up a marketing strategy. But by Thursday, you'll have collected all the information you need to do it. Then it's just a matter of sitting down and working through it. Honest.

By the time you come to draw up the marketing strategy, you'll know how to achieve your objectives in considerable detail. Which is a good thing, because a marketing strategy is not something to be woolly about. You need to be very specific about how you will achieve each objective, and to consider:

- Precisely what you will do to reach each objective
- How often you will do it
- What it will cost
- The results you expect from this action

As you can see, this is the action plan part of the document. The rest is crucial, especially if you want information, or if something is going wrong and you want to know why. But this final section of the plan is the part you will need to work from on an everyday basis.

The practicalities

So that's the information that goes into your marketing plan: where you are now, where you are going, and how you are going to get there. So what does the document actually look like? And how long will it take to write?

We'll spend Friday answering this sort of question more fully. But in general, it will probably take you a solid week or two to put the plan together from scratch. This will be reduced, of course, if you have done some of the work already, or if there is more than one of you working on it. In any case this is only a rough guide.

At the end of this, you will have a neat, clear document, smart but simply laid out, which will probably be between about ten and 25 pages long. It may be more if your business is very complex – if, for example, you sell into several very different markets.

What is the marketing plan for?

We've already seen a lot of the benefits of a marketing plan:

- It tells you things you didn't know before
- It helps you focus on areas you might otherwise miss
- It helps prevent mistakes
- It enables you to determine your critical factors for success
- It enables you to set clear marketing objectives
- It means you can work out how to achieve these objectives

These benefits should be enough in themselves to make the process of drawing up the plan worthwhile. But what are you supposed to use it for once you've finished putting it together?

For a start, you may find you need to show it to people outside the business – bank managers, potential investors, advisors, accountants, prospective business partners and so on. But you should also use it regularly as one of your most helpful business tools. You should review it regularly (we'll look at this in detail on Saturday) and it will tell you how your marketing operations are going. It will also help you spot why things have gone wrong, and enable you to put them right.

What is the difference between a marketing plan and a business plan?

One of the things that people frequently want to know is what the difference is between a marketing plan and a business plan. The answer to this is very simple. The marketing plan is part of the overall business plan. A business plan will also include a financial plan, details of administration systems, manufacturing and stock control forecasts, and so on.

Summary

Today, we've outlined what a marketing plan is, so that once you start to put it together you know what you're aiming towards.

Asking questions

We've already seen that the first thing you have to do to draw up your marketing plan is to establish where you are now. There are two stages to this: asking the right questions, and finding out the answers. Today, we're going to concentrate on the questions.

Questions to establish where you are now

- Questions about your product or service
- Questions about your customers and prospects
- Questions about your competitors
- Questions about your business

YOU ASK THE QUESTIONS

Obviously, in order to get the most out of this exercise, you're going to have to know precisely which questions to ask. So that's what we're going to look at now.

Your product or service

What exactly is it that you're marketing? You need to describe your product or service range, and every variable that it has.

No, this isn't as pointless as it may sound. We already know that outsiders (such as the bank manager) may want this information, but you may need it too. In fact, you should write it down for the very reason that it seems you shouldn't: there is a strong inclination to take it for granted.

Most companies never question the basic range they offer. But one of the strengths of a marketing plan is that everything in it is open to question whenever you review it. And often – very often – the problem with small companies that are trying to turn into large companies is that their original product range is holding them back. But they don't see it.

Example

Suppose you manage an organisation that runs training seminars and invites companies to send delegates along. As time goes by, more and more companies ask you to go along to their site and run in-house seminars for them – that's the way the trend is going.

After a while, it gets harder and harder to fill your open seminars. They start to lose you money. But you think 'We're a company that organises open seminars, we always have been. We must invest more in this side of the business so that it becomes profitable again'.

This is a mistake that companies frequently make. Perhaps you should try harder to sell your seminars. On the other hand, perhaps the market has dried up and you're pouring money into a bottomless pit. The only way you'll find out which is the case is from your marketing plan. But your marketing plan only contains the answers to the questions you asked it.

That's why you must ask every possible question. Including every possible question about your product. That way, you can be sure that if anything ever needs to change, it will show up at your marketing plan review sessions.

All right, so what are these questions you're supposed to be asking about your product or service?

Questions about the product or service range

- *What is the product or service?* What is the range? What does it look like? Does it come in a choice of colours or sizes? Are there customised options? Do you sell accessories and add-ons?

- *Where do the raw materials come from?* You might think this is a manufacturing question, and you'd be right, of course. But it's also a marketing question. Are the supplies good enough quality for your customers? Are they delivered fast enough to fulfil orders on time?
- *What is the packaging like?* Once again, this question has a marketing dimension. If your product looks basic, it won't be easy to charge a premium price for it, whatever its performance is like. And the packaging may influence the distribution, making the product too large or too heavy for certain distribution methods.

Questions about selling the product or service

- *How is the product transported?* Is transportation a problem because of cost, weight, fragility, size or anything else?
- *Where is it sold?* Direct through the post? From your own premises? Through a retailer?
- *In what form does it reach the customer?* Is it ready to use, or does it need to be assembled, painted, programmed or whatever?
- *Does it need explaining?* Will the customer understand it, or does it need instructions to go with it?
- *Is it easy to use?* Are there any integral problems that the customers might find irritating? Does it take ages to warm up, or need recharging three times a week?
- *How easy is it to increase production if sales go up?* Will you get caught out having to pay overtime you can't afford? Or sub-contracting? Or will you simply fail to deliver on time? (You can often get round these problems if they occur, but usually at a cost. That's why you need to plan for them.)

As you can see, not all these questions apply to every product or service. And there may be others that are particularly pertinent to yours. But this is a good general guide, and you should add other questions if you think of them.

Remember that you will be reviewing and updating your marketing plan regularly, so you can always add information later. But try to cover everything you can from the start.

Your customers and prospects

If you are just setting up a new business, or launching a product for a new market, you still have to ask these questions. It's just that in your case all your customers will be potential at the moment. Don't worry; tomorrow we'll find out how to get the answers to these questions even if you don't have a single customer yet.

Questions about the customers

- *Who are they?* What age? Male or female? Business or private? Where do they live? What is their income?
- *What are their buying trends?* Do they buy more or less than they used to? What about the overall market trend? Do they buy more or less if they hit hard times?
- *How much will they pay?* Would they buy more if it were cheaper? Would they pay more if it were better quality?
- *How do they know about the product or service?* Do they see it in a shop? Is it advertised? Is it reviewed in the press? Do you exhibit at trade shows?

- *Where do they buy it?* In a shop? What kind of shop? By mail order? By phone?

Questions about the customers' attitudes to the product or service

- *What do they like about your product or service?* What are the features they go for? Is it price? Accessories? After-sales service? Does the product have status value?
- *What do they dislike about it?* There must be some people who don't buy from you but from someone else. What would they say was wrong with your product or service?
- *What do they like about this type of product or service?* What are the general benefits that your product shares with the competition? (To give you an example, all people who buy electric egg whisks do so because they are faster and easier than the alternatives.)

- *What do they dislike about this type of product or service?*
- *Why do your existing customers choose your product or service rather than your competitors'?* In other words, what makes you unique?

Once again, these questions are not exhaustive, but they should give you a pretty good idea of the kind of thing you need to include in your marketing plan.

It's terribly important that you also ask the questions you might not like the answers to, such as 'what do your customers like least about your product or service?' And when it comes to finding the answers, you must be brutally honest. If your competitors are better than you in certain areas, you must acknowledge the fact. These will be some of the areas where you can generate the most improvement, but only if you recognise your shortcomings.

Your competitors

Your customers are going to judge you against your competitors constantly – and be ready to switch allegiance any time it seems worthwhile. So you had better know what they know.

This part of the plan will obviously need revising as competitors change, but for the moment you want to start with a snapshot of what the competition is up to at the moment.

Again, it's extremely important that you also ask yourself all the questions you think you might not want to hear the answers to, such as what your competitors are particularly good at. These are precisely the questions you *need* to know the answers to. Far too many business people fail because they convince themselves that they are wonderful and the competition is hopeless.

Questions about the competition

- *What product or service are your prospects using at the moment?* If they aren't buying from you yet, are they buying from someone else? Making do without? Using an alternative product? For example, if you sell electric egg whisks, do your prospects buy from a competitor, use a rotary whisk, use a fork, or not eat beaten eggs at all? What proportion of them use each of these options?
- *Who are your competitors?*
- *Do they offer anything beyond a basic service or product?* If so, what? Does their product come with extra features? Do they offer a choice of service levels?
- *What has each of your competitors got that you haven't?*

There's another useful exercise to go through when it comes to asking questions about your competitors. Draw up a table like the one on the next page. Allow as many columns as you have main competitors, plus a column for yourself. Allow enough space to fill in each section with the necessary information.

	Your product/ service	(competitor)	(competitor)
Product or service (what is the range?)			
Price (standard item for comparison)			
Special offers (what are they?)			
Quality (marks out of 10)			
Customer-care skills (marks out of 10)			
Reputation (marks out of 10)			
Delivery (marks out of 10)			
After-sales service (marks out of 10)			
Location (local, regional, national etc.)			
Advertising (what and where?)			

Your business

The final list of questions you need to draw up is about the business itself. These questions are, of course, to do with marketing, but in the broadest terms. They are questions about things that are integral to the whole business. The best way to compile this list is by using SWOT analysis.

If you haven't come across this before, it sounds horribly technical. But in fact SWOT is simply an acronym for:

- Strengths
- Weaknesses
- Opportunities
- Threats

The process of SWOT analysis involves asking yourself to describe these four factors as they apply to your business. Not how you would like them to be, but how they actually are. So let's take a look at how to do it.

The accepted way to do a SWOT analysis of your business is to draw yourself a table like the one below, and then fill in each section with a list of the appropriate points.

Strengths	Weaknesses
Opportunities	Threats

We'd better go through the four categories and explain what kind of answers you're going to need to fill in.

Strengths
The strengths and weaknesses are all to do with internal factors related to the business. You cannot have every strength there is. Being a large company can be a huge strength because it gives you a degree of financial clout that a small business can never have. On the other hand, a small company can have great speed of response and flexibility in customer handling that a multinational can't hope to achieve. You may have a broad customer base or a highly targeted customer list; you are unlikely to have both, and yet both could be strengths. So don't expect everything. Just concentrate on listing what strengths you have now.

You should list *all* your plus points in this quarter of the table – low costs, good technical knowledge or whatever.

Examples of strengths

- Low costs
- Low overheads
- Good location
- Flexibility
- Good internal communications
- Well-motivated staff
- Highly skilled staff
- Good product expertise
- Good market knowledge
- Broad customer base
- Good reputation
- Sound finances
- Up-to-date product/service range
- Up-to-date equipment
- Sophisticated computer system

Not all of these strengths will be relevant to you, and you may have others. Every business is different. But these examples should have given you a pretty good idea of the kind of things you're looking for. You'll see from this list that even if yours is a new business you may already have a number of strengths you can list.

Weaknesses
When it comes to weaknesses, you must be absolutely honest with yourself. You may think you *ought* to have a highly skilled workforce, but if you don't you must list this fact as a weakness. Otherwise it won't get on to the list of things to improve.

You will probably notice that the weaknesses are usually the other side of the 'strengths' coins. So if low costs are a strength, for example, high costs would be a weakness.

Examples of weaknesses

- High costs
- High overheads
- Poor location
- Lack of flexibility
- Poor internal communications
- Poorly motivated staff
- Poorly skilled staff
- Overdependence on one or two key staff
- Limited product expertise
- Poor market knowledge
- Small customer base
- Weak reputation

- Financially weak
- Out-of-date product/service range
- Out-of-date equipment/machinery
- Computer system that needs upgrading or replacing

Opportunities

Opportunities and threats are external market forces that impinge on your business in some way. These factors can come from all kinds of sources: customers, competitors, suppliers, EC regulations, government legislation and so on. They can even come from the media; look at the effect the BSE scandal had on the beef and dairy industries, largely because of the media interest that surrounded it.

Examples of opportunities

- Weak competition (at least in some areas)
- Competitor going out of business or moving away
- Expanding market
- New legislation in pipeline that will be good for the market
- Grants available
- Good new source of raw materials available
- Useful exhibition coming up
- New, skilled staff joining the company

Threats

As with strengths and weaknesses, threats are often the flip-side of opportunities. Only you can know exactly which areas to look at, because each business is so different. Your particular market may have special threats or opportunities that don't affect other businesses. But once again, here are some ideas.

Examples of threats

- Strong competition
- Competitor giving special offers or discounts
- Shrinking market
- New legislation in pipeline that will be bad for the market
- Grants available to competitors
- Important supplier going out of business/raw materials going up in price
- Good staff leaving the company
- Expensive legal action pending

Summary

We've looked at the questions you need to ask as soon as you start to put your marketing plan together and at how you can find out about the business itself using SWOT analysis. You may already know the answers to some of the questions we've asked. Tomorrow we'll find out how to go about answering the rest of them.

Researching the answers

Now you have a very long list of questions with no answers
to them – as yet. Today is all about researching the answers to
the questions we asked yesterday. Some of these are very
easy to answer, while others take much longer. The important
thing is not to guess at any of the answers but to do
everything you can to be sure that your answers are accurate.

There are three places you can go to for answers to your
questions, and we'll look at each one in turn:

- Off-the-shelf information
- Your customers – or potential customers, if you're
  just starting out in business
- Other people

Off-the-shelf information

The first place to find ready-made information is inside
your head. So the first thing to do is to go through the list
of questions you drew up and write down the answers to
everything you are sure you know the answer to.

This may be less than you think. Do you really know that your customers appreciate your fast delivery times? Have they ever said so? Have you ever asked them? Or read someone else's research into what matters to customers in your particular market? If not, you are only assuming the information, and you shouldn't write anything down just yet. You may well be right about how your customers feel, but we're not writing down guesses and assumptions, we're only writing down known facts.

However, you probably will know the answers to the questions about what your product range is, and about your competitors, and you'll know a lot of the answers to the SWOT analysis.

Once you've written down the answers that you are sure of at this stage, your list of questions should already be starting to look a little more manageable. There are now several places you can go to find off-the-shelf information which will give you the answers to an enormous number of questions.

Your own records
This is one of the best places to start, and one of the many reasons for keeping thorough customer records.

Assuming you're already in business, and have decent customer records, you should be able to extract all sorts of information that you hadn't realised before. For example, if you look at how your customers responded when you introduced an express delivery service – how many used it regularly, how many used it occasionally, and so on – you can start to answer the questions about delivery times.

Now you know what information you're looking for, you should be able to work out how to extract it from your records. What's more, these records of the way your customers really behave are far more reliable than anything your customers *say* they will do if, for example, you raise your prices, or introduce a fast delivery option.

Incidentally, this is also a good way to establish whether the quality of your customer records is a strength or a weakness. You can now enter that on your SWOT analysis.

Libraries
There are plenty of useful publications that any main library should have. There are also several good business libraries around the country, which your local library should be able to direct you to. Here are some of the most useful publications to look out for:

- *Yellow Pages* and *Thomson Directories*, which should give you plenty of information about potential customers, competitors and so on. Some large libraries will stock a complete set.
- *Kompass* directory lists British companies by industry, name, product and location.
- *The Source Book* organises marketing information by services and industry sectors. It will also tell you about directories, trade associations and so on.
- *Directory of British Associations* will point you towards any trade associations or societies that could help you.

- *Marketsearch* publishes around 20,000 market research reports. One of them could be just what you need.
- *BRAD (British Rate and Data)* lists every newspaper and magazine, from the trade press to local freesheets, in Britain. It gives you their distribution figures, advertising rates and so on, and will answer several of your questions about advertising.
- *Municipal Year Book* gives you a listing of local authorities including contact names.
- *The Retail Directory* lists large retail and department stores and gives the names of buyers.

Trade associations and regulatory bodies

You can often get useful information from these organisations, who publish annual reports and industry information. Some of them may charge you for this information, but if it's your own industry or a major industry for you to sell into, it could still be well worth it.

Regulatory bodies, such as the Law Society and the British Medical Association, are often good sources of information, along with trade associations. These should all be listed in some of the publications above.

Trade press

BRAD will give you listings of every trade and specialist magazine or newspaper you can imagine. Ring up the ones that are relevant to your business and ask for a copy – the advertising department will often let you have one free along with a rate card. It will be packed with information that is useful to you.

You could even ask one of the editorial staff to answer the odd question if you're really stuck and need someone with industry knowledge. They're far too busy to answer long lists of questions, but this can be a handy last resort.

Government departments
If you contact the Central Statistical Office in central London they will send you a list of government publications. You can get census reports, overseas trade information, social trends and so on. If you need information about exporting, contact your local Department of Trade and Industry office, who give very helpful advice and information.

Your local enterprise agency
This will be listed in the *Yellow Pages* under 'Business Enterprise Agencies'. Each enterprise agency is different, but they all give a wealth of advice to new and existing businesses – and it's often free. They can probably tell you about exporting, grants and loans for which you are eligible, EC legislation and plenty more.

Your customers

If you want to know what your customers and prospects think, the simplest way is to ask them. You can talk to them face-to-face, you can phone them, or you can write to them. There are three categories of customers you can talk to:

- Existing customers, to find out why they buy from you
- Potential customers, to find out what would persuade them to buy from you
- Ex-customers, to find out why they stopped buying from you

Overlaying this, you might have more than one group of customers if you sell into more than one market.

Talking to your customers face-to-face
The easiest way to do this is simply to chat to your customers informally when you are doing business with them. You could say, for example, 'We're doing a bit of research at the moment to find out how our customers feel about our delivery service. Could you tell me what you think?'

This is a cost-effective and time-effective way to research your customers, and it often generates some very useful ideas and suggestions.

On the down side, however, it's hard to build up a large sample of customers, or a long list of questions – your customers won't want to answer more than one or two off the cuff. Also, people are less likely to be honest face-to-face if their views are negative.

Overall, this is a good approach if you're only after the answers to one or two questions, or if you're looking for suggestions.

Telephoning your customers
You can always phone up customers. Tell them what you want and ask them if they can spare the time: 'Hello Mr Smith. It's Kim Jones here from ABC Ltd. We're trying to find out more about how we can improve our service to customers. I was wondering if you could spare me about five or ten minutes to answer a few questions?'

This has the advantage that you can ask more questions than you could do face-to-face, and you can make sure you ask everyone the same questions. However, it can be both expensive and time consuming if you want to research a large sample of your customers.

Generally speaking, you should use this approach when you only need to speak to a few customers, but want to ask several questions and want to be able to quantify the results.

Writing to your customers
The other option is to ask your customers to fill out a questionnaire. You can hand it out if you meet your customers regularly, or you can send it out with deliveries or bills (in which case you are only surveying customers who place orders). Alternatively, of course, you can post it.

The benefit here is that you can survey a lot of customers relatively cheaply, and you can quantify the results because you have asked them all the same questions. You can also give customers the option of remaining anonymous, which can lead to more honest replies.

General guidelines for research

There are certain fundamental mistakes that novice researchers – understandably – are inclined to make. Research is something that everyone gets better at with practice. Once you find that certain questionnaire answers aren't at all helpful, you'll learn what type of questions not to ask. So here are a few tips to help you avoid the classic pitfalls.

- *Keep your questions neutral.* If you say 'Are you happy with our delivery service?', most customers will go for the easy option and say yes. Instead ask them, for example, 'What do you think of our delivery service?'
- *Don't be ambiguous.* If you ask someone 'Do you change your car frequently?', they may think once every five years is frequently, or once every six months isn't. So ask them 'How often do you change your car?'
- *Be consistent if you want to add up the answers.* This applies if you're talking to customers face-to-face or over the phone. If you ask each customer a slightly different question, you won't be able to add up the answers properly.
- *Don't ask the customer to give up more than five or ten minutes of their time.* This applies to both telephone surveys and written questionnaires. If you have a long list of questions you want answered, you can ask one group of customers one set of questions and another group a different set. Choose the groups in a way which will divide them randomly, such as selecting them alphabetically, rather than dividing them according to location or ordering frequency.

- *Use multiple choice questions on written questionnaires.* These are much easier to analyse when you get them back. You can always mix them with other questions if you feel it would be helpful.
- *Don't expect an overwhelming response to postal questionnaires.* Somewhere between 5% and 20%, if you're mailing existing customers, is very respectable.

CAN I ASK YOU A FEW QUESTIONS?

If you want more information about conducting this kind of research, you may find another book in this series, *Successful Market Research in a week,* very helpful.

Other people

If you still have unanswered questions after looking up off-the-shelf information and talking to your customers, don't worry. There are still a few other people you can talk to.

Suppliers

Your suppliers can tell you plenty about your raw materials and other supplies. They are also often experts in their own field, which could be very useful to you.

They can tell you something about what your competitors are up to if they also supply them. Don't expect them to give away any confidences though; you wouldn't want them to tell your competitors confidential information about you. But they can probably tell you whether you get more or fewer complaints relating to their supplies, and so on.

Competitors

No, you're not expected to knock at the door and ask to go through their confidential customer records. But you can visit their shop, exhibition display stand or whatever and pick up a brochure. Or reply to their advertisements in the press.

Ring them up and ask for a copy of their annual report. If your address gives you away, use a different one. This may seem unethical, but it's normal business practice – you're only asking for publicly available material. And they're probably doing the same thing to you if they have any sense. Make a note of how fast they answer your call and send you their mailpack, and what their attitude is like on the phone.

Non-competing businesses

You can offer to swap useful information with other businesses who sell to the same market. If you sell display stands to shops, talk to someone who sells tills. You both have the same customers. If your business is local, you could phone up someone running exactly the same type of business 250 miles away, and offer to swap research information.

Advisors
Take all the advice you can, from bank managers and accountants to enterprise agencies. A lot of them are experts and can tell you a lot of what you need to know.

Filling in the blanks

You should by now have answered virtually all the questions on your original list. But there are probably a few left that you still don't have answers for. What are you supposed to do about them?

Well, if you really can't come up with an answer at the moment, you'll have to guess. At least by now you have probably reached the stage where it will be a pretty informed guess. But make it clear that it's a guess by writing 'estimate' after it in brackets or something like that. That will stop you forgetting later that the answer may not be totally accurate. You must also make yourself a note to find out the accurate answer as soon as you can.

Researching under time or budget limitations
Ideally, you should always allow yourself a few weeks at
least to put together a marketing plan. We established
earlier that it is likely to take a week or two, but this will
probably need to be spread over several weeks.

However, if you've just picked this book up because you
have to produce a marketing plan by the end of this month,
you probably don't want to hear this. If this is the case,
you'll have to put the time available into answering the
questions which fall into one of two categories:

- Questions which are very important
- Questions to which you can't even hazard an
  answer

For a new business, you should change the schedule to give yourself time to put together the fullest possible marketing plan – it's that important. But if you are producing a marketing plan for an existing business, you may find that there are a few things that it will take you a while to establish, or cost more to find out quickly than you can afford. In this case make a good guess and then start researching the answer so you can fill it in accurately as soon as possible.

Suppose you assume that your fast delivery time is important to your customers. Write that down for the time being (noting that it is 'to be confirmed'), and then start asking each customer you deal with whenever you get the chance. In a short while, you'll have enough researched answers to be able to fill in the answer properly.

And you can schedule in some time in a couple of months for doing fuller research on the other areas that need answers. Put aside time for making phone calls or drawing up a questionnaire.

Summary

You should now have written down answers to all the questions you listed on Monday and have all the information you need to put together the marketing plan. You may have had to make educated guesses at the last few questions, but most of them will be well-researched, accurate answers arrived at by using the three main sources of information.

The objectives

You have spent the last couple of days establishing where you are now. So it's time to consider where you are going with your business. That's what we'll be doing today. There are three stages in this process:

- Identify your critical success factors
- Set your objectives
- Draw up your sales forecast

This is the part many people regard as the heart of the marketing plan. In fact, the rest is just as crucial, but it's true that this section gives you direction and tells you where you should focus. Once the plan is complete, this is the part that helps you keep your eye on the ball.

You've already made things massively easier for yourself by working out where you are now, so don't be daunted by phrases like 'critical success factors' and 'sales forecast'. It's really not difficult, as we're about to find out.

Your critical success factors

These are the things you absolutely *must* do well in order for your business to be successful. They are your priorities. They could mean you have to improve your performance in any number of areas, such as:

- Reducing costs
- Improving customer service
- Speeding up lead times or delivery times
- Developing new products
- Improving quality
- Increasing the size of your customer base
- Improving after-sales service

These are just a few examples of the categories in which you might have to improve your performance. This should give you a broad picture; the specific improvement will probably be narrower than this. For example, when it comes to reducing costs, the thing that is critical to your success will probably be to reduce delivery costs, or sales costs, or whatever. You're looking for fairly precise factors.

So how do you identify your own critical success factors? You'll find all through today that you can only decide where you are going by referring to the work you've done already. And that process starts here.

On Monday, we drew up a table comparing your product and service with your main competitors' which you should have filled in by now. You are going to need to refer to this table in order to work out your critical success factors.

When you study the table, you'll see where your performance is falling significantly below your competitors'. You'll also see where everyone is scoring high or performing well – these are usually the areas that are crucial in your line of business. Perhaps everyone's prices are low, or everyone repairs faults within four hours. Have a look at this sample section from the table.

	Your product/ service	(competitor)	(competitor)
Delivery	8	6	7
After-sales service	3	4	2
Quality	4	7	8

Everybody is clearly putting a high priority on delivery, and you compare well with the rest of them. After-sales service is poor, but so is everyone else's. Perhaps this isn't too important to your customers. When it comes to quality, however, your marks are below the rest of the opposition's. They are giving it high priority – they presumably think it's important – but you don't seem to be competing well at all.

This suggests that quality is a critical success factor that you need to work on. It also suggests that delivery is a critical success factor, but in this case one that you are doing well at.

Double-check your facts
You can't rely on this table alone. But that's okay. You've done enough work already so that you don't have to. For one thing, you might know something the table doesn't –

perhaps you have a successful strategy of operating at a low quality and therefore a lower price than anyone else. If you know this works, that overrides anything the table is telling you.

You can also check this information against your customer research, from your sales records as well as from talking to customers or reading other people's research. It should confirm that quality is (or isn't) a critical factor. It should also tell you whether delivery is as important to your customers as you and your competitors seem to think. And are you all correct in thinking that after-sales service isn't important? Perhaps this is one area where you can get ahead of the field.

More often than not, your other research will bear out your competitor comparison table. But sometimes there will be differences, so it's always important to double check.

List the critical success factors
Remember that you're focusing on the *critical* factors at the moment – not all the areas where there's scope for improvement, but the ones you rely on to keep your competitive edge. List these on a separate piece of paper, because you're about to need them in order to set your objectives.

Incidentally, if you're just starting out in business you can work out the critical factors by looking at your competitors' performance alone; you should still go through this process, just leave your own performance out of the equation for now.

Your objectives

These are your statements of what you are aiming to achieve. Clearly, the critical success factors you have just listed will be top priority. These are not optional, by definition. If a factor is critical to your success, you must address it. Otherwise you can't succeed.

After that, you can go through the rest of the facts you have collected, and establish what other objectives to set yourself.

The answers to your questions about your products or services may highlight areas where you need to make improvements, such as sourcing raw materials, or packaging design.

The information about your customers should tell you whether you are missing openings in the market that you should explore, or whether there are aspects of your product design that your customers would like to see improved.

You should have established plenty of information about your competitors other than the table we've just looked at. This too will tell you which factors, while not actually critical to success, nevertheless leave room for improvement. Perhaps they have a cheaper source of raw materials than you, or lower labour costs, enabling them to keep prices down.

And your SWOT analysis will identify strengths and opportunities to exploit and weaknesses and threats to overcome.

Timescale

How far ahead are these objectives supposed to be set? Are we talking next week's plans or next year's? It varies from one business to the next, but generally speaking you should be looking a year ahead. In some businesses it will need to be longer. If you build and sell cruise liners that can take years to build, you should be looking much further ahead.

Start with a one-year plan, unless there's an obvious reason not to, and revise this if it becomes preferable to. You will be reviewing your plan regularly, as we'll see on Saturday, but every so often it will need a full update.

If you have a slack period in the year, this is a very good time to hold a regular update. This means that just before your annual update, your plan won't be looking very far ahead at all. If you need to work a year ahead all the time, update every couple of months so you have a constantly rolling marketing plan.

How to express your objectives

You need to be realistic with your objectives, but challenge yourself. You also need to be specific about what you're going to achieve.

Example

Suppose your delivery isn't as fast as the competition's. You need to improve it. Your objective should not simply state: 'To speed up delivery'.

You need to state exactly what you will aim for: 'To deliver 95% of orders within four working hours, and the remainder within six hours'.

Setting priorities

Some of your objectives can be achieved without investment. But some cannot, and you won't necessarily be able to afford to make all the necessary investments straight away. So you need to prioritise.

We've already seen that the objectives related to your critical success factors have to be addressed at once. But what about the rest of them?

Not all your objectives will relate directly to your products or services, but many of them will. If you have a fairly broad product range, you may need to decide which products to invest in first. If you get this right, you should realise a sufficient return on investment to be able to fund the next phase of objectives.

There is a very simple matrix that can help you to work out which of your products or services are most worthwhile.

High growth		
	Top priority	Average priority
	Average priority	Low priority
Low growth		
	High market share	Low market share

Allocate each of your products or services to one of these categories, according to its growth rate and its share of the market. If your company is local, this means your share of the local market for the product. As you can see, top priority should go to fast growing products with a high share of the market.

As far as your priorities for your other objectives are concerned, estimate for each one the cost of achieving it, and the potential revenue as a result of achieving it. Then grade them according to their potential profit (i.e. revenue minus cost). If you need to estimate the potential revenue you could gain by improving, say, an aspect of your after-sales service, do this on the basis of the extra sales it will earn you (or the value of the customers you now lose that you won't once the improvement is made).

Your sales forecast

The sales forecast is not the place to set yourself impossible tasks. You are supposed to be forecasting what you expect your sales to be, not what you would like them to be.

There will inevitably be more guesswork involved if you are starting up a business than if you have last year's sales figures to go on, but the principles are essentially the same.

There are several factors that you need to consider to help you estimate what your sales will be. You should by now have found out pretty much everything you can about these influences on your sales.

- *The market.* Are you selling into a growing or shrinking market? Do you know what the market trends are? Are there opportunities or threats that are likely to affect your sales?
- *The products or services.* Do your products and services have a natural shelf life? If so, take this into account. Are you planning new products? Are you aiming to introduce existing products to a wider market?

- *The competition.* What are your competitors up to? Are you likely to be competing harder for your share of the market? Or will it get easier if, say, a main competitor has gone out of business? Are you going to have to offer greater discounts or take on more staff in order to hold onto your share of the market?
- *The customers.* Are any of your large customers growing, or likely to increase their business with you? Are any of them in danger of going bust? Or moving away?
- *Contract payments.* Do you have regular large contracts? You may know that there will be a large payment every three months, say. Are you expecting to win – or lose – any large contracts in the next year?
- *Seasonal patterns.* Do your sales fluctuate through the year? If you sell beachwear, your sales will be lower in November than they will be in June.

Drawing up the forecast

Now you've gathered all your information, it really isn't that difficult to estimate what your sales are likely to be over the next year. The important thing is that you should register a profit. If you don't, it's no good tweaking the figures. You will have to adjust your entire operation until the forecast shows that you will be in profit.

The only exception to this is if you are just starting up in business. Very often it is necessary to operate at a loss for the first little while until sales have built up. In this case you should forecast up to the point where you start to show a consistent profit – even if you do have to put the last few months in pencil.

Weekly or monthly?

Most businesses forecast monthly sales, and find this sufficient. But if you're in a fast-moving market, where you have to respond quickly to new trends, you may need to forecast on a weekly basis. If you only find out once a month whether you're on target, you might have lost valuable time learning that you're behind target – time that you could have spent making changes.

What does a sales forecast look like?

A sales forecast can be just about as simple or as fancy as you like. Let's concentrate on the simple version to begin with. All you have to do is to draw up a table with the next 12 months (or 52 weeks) across the top. Down the side you list each of your products or services.

Now you simply fill in each square with the amount of sales revenue you expect from each product in that month. As you can see from the example, this allows you to add up rows or columns to calculate the total sales revenue each month, or the total revenue from each product or service over the year.

That's the basic format (as shown opposite). But there are other things that some businesses find it helpful to add. If you think they would be useful for you, add them in, or add another table to show them.

Product	Month												Total
	1	2	3	4	5	6	7	8	9	10	11	12	
A													
B													
C													
D													
E													
F													
G													
H													
Total Income													

Additional information for sales forecasts

- The number of units of each product you expect to sell
- At what (average) price you expect to sell each unit
- Income earned and cash due as separate entries, especially where payment may be slow or delayed
- Sales of each product to each customer type, where you are selling into more than one market
- Sales by geographical location

For sales by product, location or anything other than month or week, it's best to draw up a separate forecast for each month. You can view this alongside your overall basic forecast for the year.

Summary

Not only do we know where we are at the moment, but now we know where we're going as well.

The important thing is to work out what needs to be done, concentrating especially on those things that are absolutely essential for success.

Then you have to determine where you are going. Set yourself challenges, but make them realistic ones, and draw up a sales forecast based on what you expect your sales to look like, not some fantasy of what you would like them to be.

Once you've done all that, you're ready to go on to the last stage of preparation – working out how to get from where you are to where you're going.

Converting objectives into action plans

The final stage of preparation, before you finally commit
your plan to paper, is to work out how you're going to get
from where you are to where you're going – your route map.

There are three steps you have to go through to convert
each of your objectives (from yesterday) into a marketing
strategy, or action plan:

- Look at the options
- Consider the practicalities
- Select the best route

You've already established that your objectives are
achievable – if challenging – so you know it's all possible.
Every one of your objectives can generate a workable action
plan. So let's look at the best way to do it.

Look at the options

You should have a list of your objectives, and you need to go through each one in turn. Treat each one separately, and go through the process in this chapter to put together a mini action plan for each one. When you've finished, all these action plans together will make up your marketing strategy.

For most of the objectives you have set, you'll find there are a number of ways you might achieve them. Let's take the example that you're trying to reduce your delivery times to under four working hours. There are several (feasible) ways you might do this:

* Contract out all your deliveries to someone else
* Change your working system so orders are processed faster, drivers check in more frequently, and so on
* Employ more drivers

You might well come up with more options if you're in this situation. For the moment, simply write down the possibilities. We'll worry about how to pick the right one in a minute.

The important thing is to think as freely as possible to make sure you consider everything that might be useful. This is a process in which imaginative thinking and open-minded approach are valuable. Try to brainstorm ideas for this with other people if you can; it's an excellent way to generate ideas.

There are more methods than can possibly be listed here for improving every aspect of your marketing. But it is possible to give you an idea of the kinds of activities to think about. These can be broadly divided into five main marketing areas. Most of your objectives will fall into one of these categories:

Five key areas of marketing

- Increase awareness of your company and your products/services
- Increase existing customers' loyalty
- Secure sales
- Generate higher turnover
- Increase your knowledge of your market

We can take each of these in turn and list the type of options you should be considering. However, don't be tempted to think that these lists are exhaustive. Be open to thinking up other approaches for achieving your objectives as well.

Increase awareness of your company and your products/services

- Advertising – local and national press, trade press, radio, TV
- Press releases – in the local, national or trade press
- Direct mail – using your own mailing list, bought list, rented lists
- Exhibitions
- Sales promotions
- Telephone selling

- Personal sales visits
- Customer/prospect newsletter
- Special events
- Sponsorship

Increase existing customers' loyalty

- Improve customer care
- Make more contacts with customers
- Give customers a single point of contact
- Improve delivery
- Improve product quality
- Improve after-sales service
- Improve accuracy of billing

Secure sales

- Close the sale on a higher percentage of visits/phone calls
- Improve quality/range of brochures and other sales literature
- Get customer's signature on contract/deposit earlier in process
- Improve sales training for staff

Generate higher turnover

- Increase sales on certain products and services
- Launch new products and services
- Increase prices
- Concentrate on the most profitable product lines
- Employ more sales staff

- Use sales agents
- Open new branches
- Enter new markets
- Sell regionally as well as locally, or nationally as well as regionally
- Start exporting, or expand your exporting operations

Increase your knowledge of your market

- Run customer surveys
- Hold customer forums
- Subscribe to trade journals
- Conduct your own research
- Commission market research
- Buy in ready-made research
- Talk to suppliers
- Research competitors
- Form partnerships with non-competing businesses

Not every one of these approaches will work for every option, of course. But you will usually find there's more than one way to achieve your objectives.

Making it more specific

These are only broad approaches, of course. They are not the whole story. Each one of them still begs several questions which need answering. Let's look at a few examples.

- *Exhibiting.* This is one way to increase awareness, but your objective will have been more specific. It will have said, for example, 'To increase awareness of our products among business customers in the tourism industry'. So your options for achieving it must be more specific too. You'll need to suggest which exhibitions you should attend, what stand you should use, which staff should attend and so on.
- *Commissioning market research.* Again, this will increase your market knowledge, but you'll need to be more specific. What sort of research will you commission? Questionnaires in the post? People with clipboards on street corners? Who do you intend to survey? What sort of information are you aiming to get from it? From whom will you commission the research?
- *Secure sales by improving staff training.* Which staff? How much training? In what areas? In-house or external training?
- *Make more contacts with customers.* By post, phone or face-to-face? How often? For what purpose?

So to recap:

Look at the options

- Take each objective one at a time
- Brainstorm a choice of approaches you could take to achieve it
- Make each suggestion as specific as you can

Consider the practicalities

Now that you have a list of objectives, each with a choice of ways to achieve it, you need to start finding out which approach is best in each case.

The way to do this is to examine the implications of each option from a practical point of view. In each case you need to calculate:

- *The potential revenue* from achieving the objective using this method.
- *The cost* of using this method.
- *The time implications* – how long will it take to achieve it and when could you start – in other words what would the schedule be?
- The implications for *staffing* – could it be done by the existing staff, or would you need to bring in experienced people or contract out? (This obviously has an impact on your costs as well.)

- Will you need to run any *training* in order to put this approach into operation? How long will it take? Do you have suitable staff who could be trained up effectively?
- Are there any *transport* implications? Would you have to commit to more deliveries? Or start shipping overseas? Or increase your fleet size?

You should have enough information to be able to do these calculations quite easily. Then you'll be ready to weigh options against each other. If any of your calculations show that a particular option isn't going to be cost effective, either revise it or abandon it.

Select the best route

You should find that by the time you've identified all the feasible options, and then considered the practical implications of each one, it isn't difficult to choose the best way to meet your objectives.

Occasionally, you'll find that there really isn't much to choose between two or more of the options. If this is the case, don't waste time over the decision of which option to take. If either will do the job equally well, pick either. It probably doesn't matter.

There is one thing, however, that you must consider: combining options. This often results in the best of all worlds. Take our example of reducing delivery times to under four working hours. If you remember, we identified three basic options for doing this:

- Contract out all your deliveries to someone else
- Change your working system so orders are processed faster, drivers check in more frequently, and so on
- Employ more drivers

These options are not mutually exclusive. Once you've weighed up the practicalities, consider mixing some of the options. For example:

- Change your working system but *also* contract out some deliveries at peak times
- Change your system *and* employ a part-time driver from 2 p.m. to 4 p.m. each afternoon

When it comes to objectives that relate to increasing awareness of your company, or your products or services, you'll find that there are often several approaches that will work. They can frequently be mixed, and often they will support each other if you mix them to give you a better result than they ever could alone.

For example, you can combine direct mailshots with telephone selling to excellent effect – the combined approach will give better results than either could on its own. Or you can support an appearance at an exhibition with advertising in the trade press. Or you can run several awareness campaigns quite independently of each other, such as a feature article in the local paper, a trade exhibition and a telemarketing campaign. This last approach would be particularly suitable if you need to increase awareness in several distinct markets.

Budgeting
Once you have decided which options to choose, it should be fairly straightforward to calculate the cost of meeting each objective. You've already costed each option, after all.

All you have to do is add up the individual costs of meeting all the objectives, and you have your overall marketing budget. You already know how much revenue you expect it to generate, and that it will more than pay for itself.

It will sometimes happen, nevertheless, that you simply can't afford to invest this much at once, until you've started to see some return. In this case you will need to go back and revise the options.

If you can't reduce the costs, put some of the lower-priority objectives on hold until the increased revenue from the first few is available to pay for them.

In this case, budget in this revenue, and also show in your budget that you will be reinvesting this revenue once you have it – later in the year – to put your other strategies into practice.

At the end of all this, you should have a clear list of objectives, with your action plan for meeting each one. This will not only outline how you will meet the objective, but will also give a schedule for doing so.

Summary

That's really all there is to it. You simply take each objective, look at where you are now, and then work out how to get from one to the other.

First, work out what your options are. Then take into account the practicalities:

- Cost
- Time
- Staffing
- Training
- Transport

Then choose the best route based on this information.

Consider the possibility of combining two or more options. Then draw up a budget and, if necessary, revise your strategy to fit your overall budget. Once you have selected and listed these action points, you have drawn up your marketing strategy.

You've now done all the serious hard work you need to in order to draw up your marketing plan. All that's left is to put the whole lot together on paper.

Putting the plan together

Congratulations. You've done all the thinking work. Now you simply have to put your plan down on paper in the right order. This is a fairly straightforward process which will get you from the huge pile of material and notes on your desk, to a few smartly presented pages which are easy to understand.

Putting the plan together

- Assemble your data and review the plan as a whole
- Establish the content
- Plan the design and layout
- Write it up clearly and simply

The aim is to end up with a document that you can work from efficiently, and which you would be proud to show your bank manager or any other outsider to whom you need to show it.

Assemble your data and review the plan as a whole

The first thing you need to do is to collect together all the finalised information for your marketing plan. Not the books and documents you used to research it, not the lists of notes; just the answers, so to speak:

- Answers to the questions we asked on Monday
- Competitor comparison table
- SWOT analysis
- Objectives
- Sales forecast
- Marketing strategy

Keep the rest of your notes and research data – survey results or whatever – in a safe place. You never know when you may want to refer back to them, so don't throw them away.

Now have a look through the material you've still got on your desk. It's a good idea to do this after you've had a break from the detailed work of planning the strategy – the next morning is a good time for it. The aim is to give yourself an overview of the whole thing.

You may find when you do this that a couple of things don't quite fit together, or there's something important in the early research that has somehow failed to make its way into the objectives or strategy. Or there might be an important question you couldn't answer at the time that you now feel you can. So this is your chance to review the plan as a whole, rather than looking at it in bits, as you have done up to now.

Establish the content

The next step is to work out what is going to go into the final plan. Don't get upset at leaving out things that you spent ages working on. For one thing, you needed to do the work in order to arrive at a really effective plan. And for another thing, you'll keep the material for reference and – as you'll see in the next chapter – there'll be plenty of opportunities to refer back.

Also, you may find that the bank manager or the shareholders or someone may want more background detail on certain aspects of the plan. That's when you'll be able to produce from the filing cabinet all these extra documents that never made it to the final document.

So what is going to find its way into the final plan? Well some things are compulsory and some are optional. There is a list of things – which we'll look at in a moment – that really have to be there; everyone expects it. But that doesn't mean that everything else is banned.

You want to keep the document as brief as you can – between about ten and 25 pages – but if there's other information which in your case you feel is particularly important, then you can include it.

As for the compulsory information, the following things should always find their way into the finished plan:

Core contents of the marketing plan

Where your business is now:

- Key facts about your products or services
- Key facts about the customers

- Key facts about the competition (including the comparison table)
- SWOT analysis

Where your business is going:

- Your objectives
- Your sales forecast

How your business is going to get there:

- Your marketing strategy

You'll notice that you only need to include the key facts about your products or services, your customers and your competitors. Only you will know precisely what these are.

The point is that once you've answered some of your early questions, you'll find that some of the answers repeat each other, and some of the information turns out – once you have it – to be less relevant than it might have been. So you won't necessarily need to reproduce the full list of answers that you researched.

You should be able to judge this for yourself and, if in doubt, keep the information in there. You can always put it in an appendix at the back so it's out of the way for anyone who doesn't need to read it.

As well as the core contents of the marketing plan, there are one or two other practical inclusions you need to make, to render it easier to read and to use.

Other contents of the marketing plan

- Cover page – stating company name, address, phone number and the date the plan was prepared; also give your own name and phone number
- Contents page
- Summary (we'll look at this in more detail in a moment)
- Appendices – if you think it would help to include some of your extra information in an appendix

The first three of these – cover page, contents and summary – should go at the beginning, in that order. The summary is extremely important. It may not matter much to you – you know what's in the document anyway – but if you have to show your marketing plan to the bank manager, potential investors and so on, they may well decide whether or not to read the whole plan purely on the basis of the summary.

So you need to know what goes into the summary. Everything in the document, really, but in brief. Just give the results of key points from each section:

- Where you are now – include a brief description of the products, type of customers and key competitors. Give the most crucial one or two strengths and opportunities. Since the summary is usually for people who you are hoping will invest, lend or whatever, it's best not to call attention to your weaknesses at this point. They need to be included in the plan – it wouldn't be credible without them, and a smart investor will spot them anyway – but they don't need to go into the summary.

- Where you are going – summarise your key objectives and give the bottom line of the sales forecast; don't bother with the monthly or weekly breakdown.
- How you are going to get there – again, summarise your strategy, and don't give the detailed specification of each action point, just the first stage you went through. So you can say that you will 'increase your customer base by 30% through advertising and exhibitions' without giving details of which exhibitions you plan to attend, and so on.

As far as the length is concerned, the point of the summary is to give a brief précis, so you need to keep it short. Aim to keep it to one sheet of paper, but if the whole document is long, you may have to run over onto a second sheet.

Although the summary goes at the beginning, you will no doubt have realised for yourself that the sensible thing is to write it last. If you do this, you'll find it far quicker and easier.

Incidentally, you'll probably find it a very helpful mental exercise as well. It tends to focus the mind on the absolutely central issues in a way that can give you a much clearer vision of where you're leading your business.

Plan the design and layout

We've already seen that the finished document should be between about ten and 25 pages long – nearer ten for a small business. This may seem rather long, and the reason for this is simply that if you want to impress people with your plan, you need to present it professionally and clearly.

And to do that takes up more space than presenting it badly. You could cram the plan into four or five pages, but it would look impenetrable and be hard to read.

So let's take a look at the most important rules of layout and presentation for creating a smart, professional document.

Packaging
The first thing to consider is the packaging. You don't want to present someone with a few stapled pieces of paper and tell them it's your marketing plan. But at the other extreme, you shouldn't have it leather bound with your company name engraved on the cover in gold leaf. Apart from anything else, this gives the impression that the contents are likewise engraved – in stone. A marketing plan is a flexible document and it should give that impression.

By far the best approach is to use a good-quality laser or inkjet printer, and print out your plan on good-quality, plain white paper (not laid paper, which is the finely textured paper often used for letterheads – it doesn't take print so well).

Then have the whole thing bound with, for instance, a spiral binding and a clear plastic cover front and back. That will look smart and professional but not over the top.

Space
Your marketing plan will look much better, and be easier for you and anyone else to read and use, if you double space it and use reasonably wide margins. It will look more professional if you justify the text (in other words, line up the right-hand ends of the lines). This will also help to focus the eye on the text, which makes it look more important.

Make it easy to follow

Having included a contents list, you will naturally number the pages to help other people find their way around the marketing plan. You will also need to include clear headings and sub-headings to make sure the reader can find the section they are looking for. This also has the benefit of breaking the text up a little more so that it looks readable and approachable.

Keep it simple

Limit yourself to two fonts (types of lettering) for the whole document. Use one for headings and one for text. Or stick to just one throughout if you like. You can use different sizes, bold, italics and so on, but only in moderation.

The aim is to produce a document that is clean, readable and easy to follow. You're supposed to be exercising your marketing skills, not your prowess as a designer. Fussy or fancy designs distract the reader from the content, which is the part that matters in a marketing plan.

Make sure any tables, such as the sales forecast, or competitor comparison table, are neat and simple. A page of text with tables or charts on it quickly looks confusing and messy if the graphics are at all fussy.

So don't play around with loads of different line thicknesses and typefaces. Just use bold type for column and row headings and keep the whole thing as simple as possible.

By the same token, don't start showing off with clever icons or bits of clipart. By all means put your logo on the title page, and perhaps even at the very end if there's a lot of the last page left blank, but leave it at that.

Write it up clearly and simply

Now that you have a smart-looking, well-presented marketing plan that contains all the essential information, the only thing left is to make sure that whoever you show it to can read it.

There are a few guidelines worth following to make sure that your style is clear and easy to follow, and that people enjoy reading your plan. If the language is convoluted or over-complicated, it can be so hard to work out what the individual words and sentences mean that it becomes impossible to take in the overall meaning of the document.

Guidelines for writing clear English

- Use ordinary, everyday language – don't try to be clever
- Use short words
- Use short sentences – average 20 words and don't exceed 40
- Use short paragraphs – they should never look deeper than they are wide
- Don't use jargon that your readers might not be familiar with
- Avoid legal terms and pompous words – such as 'herewith' and 'therein'
- Use active rather than passive verbs – make the subject of the sentence do something rather than have it done to them: *The boss phoned me* rather than *I was phoned by the boss*
- Use concrete rather than abstract nouns – abstract nouns often end with '-tion': write *car* rather than *transportation.*

Summary

You've completed your marketing plan. Today we've worked through the four stages of putting the plan together. First of all we assembled the data and reviewed the plan as a whole – the first proper opportunity for an overview of the work you've done up to now. Then we looked at the three stages of transferring the work to the final document.

Establish the contents
First of all, establish what exactly is going into the report. There are the core contents, that set out where you are now, where you are going and how you are going to get there. And then there are the other ingredients – the cover page, contents, summary and, sometimes, appendices.

Plan the design and layout
Next we looked at the packaging and design of the marketing plan. We established that it should be presented in a way that looks smart and professional but not over the top. Then we looked at how to use space, page numbers and headings, and the importance of keeping the design really simple.

Write it up clearly and simply
Finally we considered the importance of using simple, everyday language so that the document is easy to read and take in. We looked at the most important guidelines for writing clear English, such as keeping words, sentences and paragraphs short.

So now you have your completed marketing plan, and all that's left is to make sure you get the most out of it. After all, you want to make all the work that's gone into it worthwhile — and it will be.

Using the marketing plan

We've spent the last few days putting together a marketing plan from scratch, and you should now have a smart document sitting neatly on your desk. So this is a good time to recap everything we did to get here.

Drawing up a successful marketing plan

- Asking the right questions
- Researching the answers
- Setting the objectives and sales forecast
- Planning the marketing strategy
- Putting it all together

It hasn't been difficult, but it's taken a fair bit of work and it seems a shame to waste it. So the last thing we're going to do today – but by no means the least important – is to find out what you're supposed to do with the damn thing now you've got it.

Asking the right questions

On Monday, we had a look at the first stage of the marketing plan: drawing up a list of questions. The important thing is to ask the right questions so you end up collecting all the information you're going to need later.

We established that there are four areas you need to ask questions about:

- Your product or service
- Your customers
- Your competitors
- Your business

To begin with, you have to specify exactly what it is that you're marketing. If you never focus on this, you'll never notice if it needs to change. We looked at some of the most important questions to ask:

Questions about the product or service

- What is the product or service?
- Where do the raw materials come from?
- What is the packaging like?
- How is the product transported?
- Where is it sold?
- In what form does it reach the customer?
- Does it need explaining?
- Is it easy to use?
- How easy is it to increase production if sales go up?

Next, we examined the sort of questions you need to ask about your customers and potential customers. Of course, if you're just starting out in business, all of your customers will be potential.

We discussed the importance of asking yourself uncomfortable questions, such as 'What do your customers dislike about your product?' Only by investigating these areas will you really learn what you need to know about how you can keep improving your business.

Questions about the customers

- Who are they?
- What are their buying trends?
- How much will they pay?
- How do they know about the product or service?
- Where do they buy it?
- What do they like about your product or service?
- What do they dislike about it?
- What do they like about this type of product or service?
- What do they dislike about this type of product or service?
- Why do your existing customers choose your product or service rather than your competitors'?

The next area we asked questions about was the competition. You need to check out any other business that your potential customers might go to instead of buying from you. They may not be selling the same product – it could be a competing type of product. If you sell electric egg whisks, companies selling rotary whisks are competing with you.

Questions about the competition

- What product or service are your prospects using at the moment?
- Who are your competitors?
- Do they offer anything beyond a basic product or service, and if so, what?
- What has each of your competitors got that you haven't?

We also drew up a table of comparison with your competitors. We listed you and your competitors across the top, and the various factors to compare down the side. This gives you an at-a-glance picture of where you are doing well or badly against the rest of the field.

Lastly, we asked questions about the business, which we did using SWOT analysis.

Lists to draw up using SWOT analysis

- Strengths
- Weaknesses
- Opportunities
- Threats

Researching the answers

On Tuesday, we researched the answers to all these questions. We found there were three places you could go for information:

- Off-the-shelf information
- Your customers and potential customers
- Other people

Off-the-shelf information

- Your own records
- Libraries
- Trade associations and regulatory bodies
- Trade press
- Government departments
- Your local enterprise agency

Your customers

- Existing customers
- Potential customers
- Ex-customers

You can get information from customers by talking to them, phoning them or writing to them, and we looked at the pros and cons of all these approaches.

Other people

- Suppliers
- Competitors
- Non-competing businesses
- Advisors

Setting the objectives and sales forecast

Once you've collected all your information together, you need to do something with it. You've already established, by answering the lists of questions, where your business is now. So it's time to work out where it's going.

Identify your critical success factors
Go through the answers which you now have, and identify which factors are absolutely vital to your success. These are the things without which your business cannot thrive.

First of all, go through your competitor comparison table and see where your performance is falling short of the average. Then see where everyone, including you, is scoring highly. These are the areas that are likely to be critical. Check these against other answers if you're sceptical and, once you're satisfied, note them down as critical factors.

The weaknesses and threats in your SWOT analysis are also worth checking through, to see if they bear out any other indicators of where you absolutely must improve your performance. They are not an answer in themselves, because not every weakness is crucial, or even avoidable.

Establish your objectives
Now you need to set yourself objectives based on the areas where you need to improve. Top of the list should be your critical success factors. You'll also want to look through your other information as well to work out what needs to be done.

In general, you're setting yourself objectives for the next year. However, in some cases you may be aiming to achieve a certain thing much faster than that, or to reach a particular objective over several years.

Each objective should be specific, so you know exactly what you're aiming at. Don't aim *'To speed up delivery'*; aim *'To deliver 95% of orders within four working hours, and the remainder within six hours'.*

We also looked at how to set priorities if you can't afford either the money, or the time, to pursue all your objectives straight away.

Draw up your sales forecast
This is a forecast of what you expect your sales to be, not a fantasy of what you'd like them to be. There are half a dozen factors, other than your sales figures for last year, that you should take into account to help you estimate your sales as accurately as possible.

Factors that will help you estimate sales

- The market
- The products or services
- The competition
- The customers
- Contract payments
- Seasonal patterns

Planning the marketing strategy

The final stage of preparation involves converting your objectives into action plans. In other words, having established where you are now, and where you are going, this is the time to establish how you are going to get from A to B. The three main stages to achieving this are:

- Look at the options
- Consider the practicalities
- Select the best routes

Look at your options
You need to examine, for each objective, all the plausible options you can think of for achieving it. We looked at the kind of approaches you should consider within each of the five main areas of marketing that your objectives are likely to fit into:

- Increasing awareness of your company and your products/services
- Increasing existing customers' loyalty
- Securing sales
- Generating higher turnover
- Increasing your knowledge of your market

Look at your options

- Take each objective one at a time
- Brainstorm a choice of aproaches you could take to achieve it
- Make each suggestion as specific as you can

Consider the practicalities
The next stage in drawing up your marketing strategy is to look at the practical implications of each option. You need to consider several aspects.

Practical considerations

- Potential revenue
- Cost
- Time implications
- Staffing
- Training
- Transport

Select the best route
It should be fairly clear which of the options you identified is going to be the most effective. If there's nothing to choose, it doesn't matter which you go for. Bear in mind the possibility of combining options; this can work very well. We considered one or two ways in which you could do this.

Finally, we looked at the budgeting for your marketing plan. Once you've added up the costs of all the options you plan to adopt, you have a budget. Sometimes you really can't afford to launch into all these marketing schemes straight away. So we finished by looking at what you do if this is the case. By the end of Thursday we had a list of objectives, with a costed and scheduled action plan for achieving each one.

Putting it all together

On Friday, we pulled everything together into a finished document. We started by assembling all the data we were going to put into it, and then reviewing it all together, to make sure there was no repetition or inconsistency. Then we established the precise contents of the final document.

Establish the contents

- Cover page
- Contents page
- Summary
- Where you are now:
  key facts about your products or services
  key facts about your customers
  key facts about your competitors
  SWOT analysis
- Where you are going:
  your objectives
  your sales forecast
- How you are going to get there:
  your marketing strategy
- Appendices (if you need them)

After that, we looked at the key points of layout and design, including packaging, spacing, page numbering and headings. We also established the importance of keeping the design clear and simple.

Finally, we looked at the guidelines for writing clear English, using short words, sentences and paragraphs.

Using your marketing plan

And finally … What are you going to do with this marketing plan? You're going to wring every last drop of value from it, that's what. And you will be able to derive plenty of benefits from it if you use it wisely.

You've already learnt a huge amount doing it, and come up with strategies you would never have arrived at without it. You also have a professional and thorough document you can show to anyone who needs to see it, from your bank manager to consultants, investors and incoming directors.

But you don't want to frame it and hang it on the wall, looking impressive, as a memento of all your hard work. You can get far more value from it as a working document that you refer to regularly.

Implement the plan
For a start, you will need to implement the strategies that you have set in the plan. You've written yourself an action plan with a schedule and a budget, so you can start putting it into practice.

Update the plan
You'll remember that we started with a list of questions which we researched the answers to. There were probably a few answers that you couldn't find at the time and had to make an educated guess at. Well, you can fill some of them in as you go along.

This is worth doing for two reasons. For one thing, you may have guessed wrong, and the right answers might affect your strategy so you need to know about them in order to keep it up to date.

The other reason is that if you keep your marketing plan regularly updated, you will never have to go through the work of putting it together from scratch again. If you let it sit at the back of a filing cabinet for five years, it will be virtually useless at the end of that time. If you need it then, you'll have to start again.

So make yourself an action point to fill in the guesstimate questions as soon as you can. Be on the lookout for the information you need.

You should also schedule an update session (with action points) every so often. Once a year is enough for a lot of companies. If your business or market is changing fast, once every six months might be better. You should make a point of checking every fact to see whether it needs updating. Your product range may have changed, or a new supplier may have arrived on the market. Most facts may not need altering, but if you don't consciously check, you'll miss something.

Take your competitor comparison chart as an example.
Have any new competitors arrived on the scene? Has one
of your competitors revamped and improved their
approach to customer care? Are you still doing as well by
comparison with the rest of the field? If not, are you doing
better or worse?

Review the plan
You also need to review the plan – again, once a year is
usually sufficient but you might want to make it more
frequent. Do this shortly after you have updated it.

If you have achieved the objectives you set out last year,
you are going to need a new set of objectives, and a new
strategy to achieve them. Many businesses take a couple of
days out for their directors or senior managers to get
together and hammer out next year's plan. But you could
set aside a long session every few months if that suits you
better.

Your update will tell you about any changes in the market,
your customers' attitudes, your product, the competition,
your strengths and weaknesses, and so on. These will help
you devise a new set of objectives, using the same approach
as for the original plan.

Use the plan proactively
Keep using the plan to generate ideas. Look at the SWOT
analysis and ask yourself if there's anything else you could
be doing to build on your strengths, or make the most of
opportunities.

When things go wrong, use the plan to tell you why. Suppose you start missing your sales targets. The odds are that you'll be able to work out why if you look through your marketing plan. And you'll be able to find a way to get back on target.

Suppose the reason you're missing your targets is because a new competitor has arrived on the scene. Don't give in – fight. Update your competitor comparison table and use it to help you brainstorm ways to maintain and build your share of the market.

So you see, a marketing plan isn't a tedious document you're obliged to prepare to keep the bank manager happy. It's one of the most useful business tools you'll ever lay your hands on, and the more you learn to use it, the more indispensible you will find it.

For information

on other

IN A **WEEK** titles

go to

www.inaweek.co.uk